Celebrations in My World

Juneteenth

Lynn Peppas

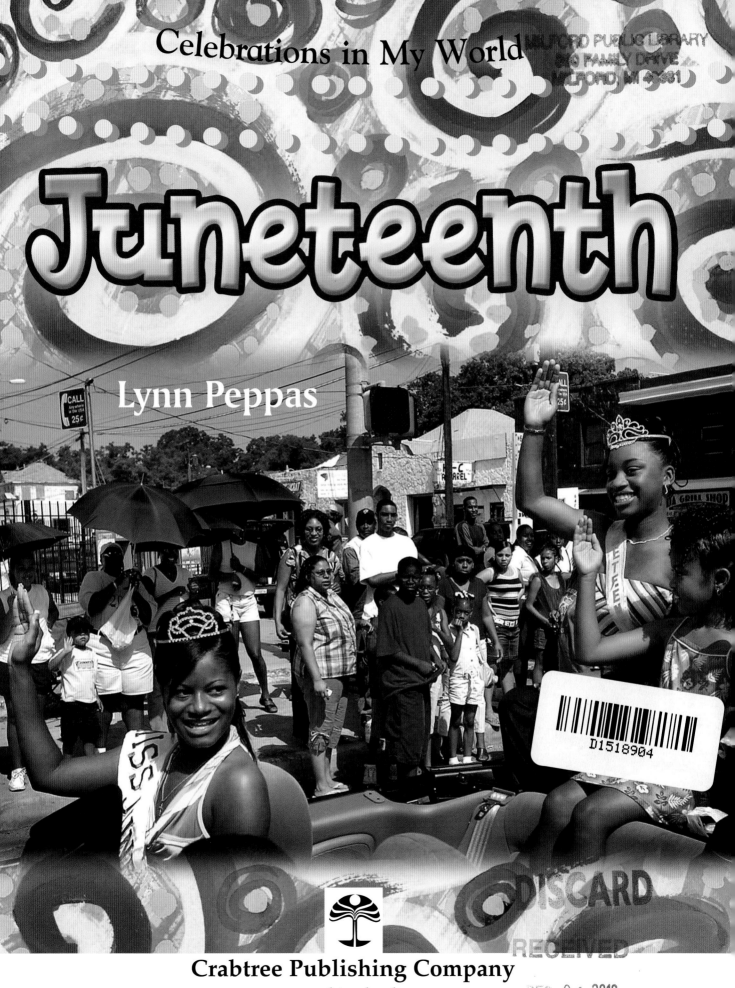

Crabtree Publishing Company
www.crabtreebooks.com

Crabtree Publishing Company
www.crabtreebooks.com

Author: Lynn Peppas
Coordinating editor: Chester Fisher
Series and project editor: Susan LaBella
Editor: Adrianna Morganelli
Proofreader: Reagan Miller
Photo research: Crystal Sikkens
Editorial director: Kathy Middleton
Design: Katherine Berti
Suzena Samuel (Q2AMEDIA)
**Production coordinator and
Prepress technician:** Katherine Berti

Illustrations:
Barbara Bedell: pages 8, 9
Margaret Amy Salter: page 4

Photographs:
Alamy: Jeff Greenberg: pages 23, 27; A. T. Willett: page 26
Associated Press: page 21
BigStockPhoto: page 24
Dreamstime: page 17
iStockPhoto: pages 6, 18, 29, 30
Keystone Press: Dan McDuffie: page 22
Photolibrary: North Wind Picture Archives: page 7
WpN/UPPA/Photoshot: pages 1, 14, 15, 25
Shutterstock: pages 5, 10, 11, 12, 16, 19, 20, 31
Bob Daemmrich/The Image Works: cover (except
    Emancipation Proclamation)
Wikipedia: Engraving by W. Roberts: cover (Emancipation
    Proclamation); Mathew Brady: page 13; Nsaum75: page 28

Library and Archives Canada Cataloguing in Publication

Peppas, Lynn
    Juneteenth / Lynn Peppas.

(Celebrations in my world)
Includes index.
Also issued in an electronic format.
ISBN 978-0-7787-4928-8 (bound).--ISBN 978-0-7787-4935-6 (pbk.)

    1. Juneteenth--Juvenile literature. 2. Slaves--Emancipation--
Texas--Juvenile literature. 3. African Americans--Texas--
Galveston--History--Juvenile literature. 4. African Americans--
Anniversaries, etc.--Juvenile literature. 5. African Americans--Social
life and customs--Juvenile literature. 6. Slaves--Emancipation--
United States--Juvenile literature. I. Title. II. Series: Celebrations
in my world

E185.93.T4P46 2010   j394.263   C2010-902751-5

Library of Congress Cataloging-in-Publication Data

Peppas, Lynn.
    Juneteenth / Lynn Peppas.
        p. cm. -- (Celebrations in my world)
    Includes index.
    ISBN 978-0-7787-4935-6 (pbk. : alk. paper) -- ISBN 978-0-7787-4928-8
(reinforced library binding : alk. paper) -- ISBN 978-1-4271-9445-9
(electronic (pdf))
    1. Juneteenth--Juvenile literature. 2. Slaves--Emancipation--Texas--
Juvenile literature. 3. African Americans--Texas--Galveston--History--
Juvenile literature. 4. African Americans--Anniversaries, etc.--Juvenile
literature. 5. African Americans--Social life and customs--Juvenile
literature. 6. Slaves--Emancipation--United States--Juvenile literature.
I. Title. II. Series.

    E185.93.T4P47 2010
    394.263--dc22
                                            2010016406

Crabtree Publishing Company

Printed in China/082010/AP20100512

www.crabtreebooks.com   1-800-387-7650

Published in Canada
Crabtree Publishing
616 Welland Ave.
St. Catharines, Ontario
L2M 5V6

Published in the United States
Crabtree Publishing
PMB 59051
350 Fifth Avenue, 59th Floor
New York, New York 10118

Published in the United Kingdom
Crabtree Publishing
Maritime House
Basin Road North, Hove
BN41 1WR

Published in Australia
Crabtree Publishing
386 Mt. Alexander Rd.
Ascot Vale (Melbourne)
VIC 3032

Contents

What Is Juneteenth?

Juneteenth is an American holiday that celebrates people's **freedom** from slavery in the United States. Slaves were people who had no freedom. They were made to work hard for no pay.

- Often, slaves were forced to work long hours with very few breaks.

DID YOU KNOW?

Juneteenth is a word that is made up of two words: June and nineteenth. Put them together and you get Juneteenth!

- Look for Juneteenth on a calendar.

Juneteenth is celebrated on June 19. Some states celebrate it on the third Saturday in June.

On Juneteenth, Americans from all different backgrounds remember the African Americans' struggle for freedom.

Families and friends get together to share cookouts. They listen to speeches and learn about African-American history.

5

Atlantic Slave Trade

For many thousands of years, people have forced other people to do their work for them as slaves. This happened in the United States when people settled there more than 500 years ago.

African people were forced onto ships to sail to America to become slaves.

DID YOU KNOW?

*Ships sailing to America were **overcrowded**. Some African people did not **survive** the trip.*

Ship owners from **Europe** sailed to Africa and bought people from African traders. Men, women, and children were taken to be slaves.

The slaves crossed the Atlantic Ocean from Africa to America on large sailing ships. The trip took many weeks. It was called the Atlantic Slave Trade.

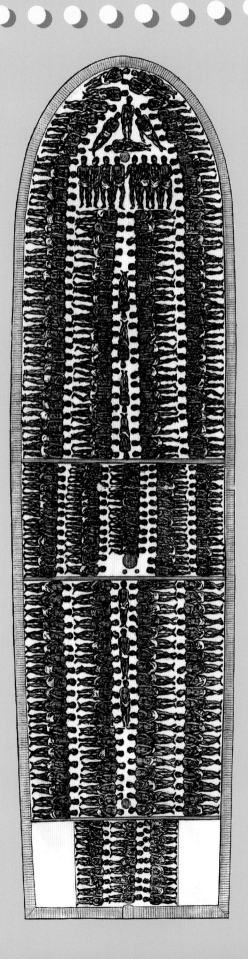

• The ships were arranged to fit as many people as possible.

7

African Americans

African people were taken away from their homes and families. They were kept like prisoners and sold to people living in the United States. There, they were made to work on farms called **plantations**, or in homes.

- Slaves of all ages could be seen working in cotton fields.

DID YOU KNOW?

Millions of Africans were brought to the United States to become slaves.

Children of slaves were also expected to work for their owners.

They spent long hours working in the fields, or doing cooking and cleaning in their owners' homes.

Many slaves raised families who also became slaves. They were born in America but their **ancestors** were from Africa.

9

American Civil War

Many Americans believed that slavery was wrong. Some American states, called free states, did not allow slavery. Some states did allow slavery. America was split into these two groups.

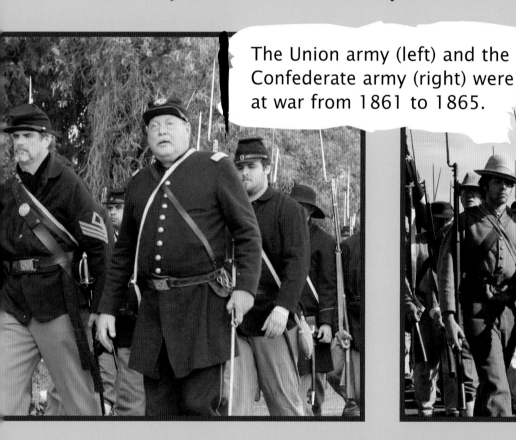

The Union army (left) and the Confederate army (right) were at war from 1861 to 1865.

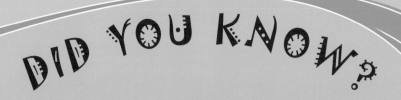

The Union won the American Civil War on May 26, 1865.

10

Hundreds of thousands of people died during the American Civil War.

The group against slavery was the Union. It was supported by 25 northern states. The group for slavery was the Confederacy. The Confederate army was made up of 11 southern states. The two groups went to war in 1861. This war is called the American Civil War.

The First Juneteenth

President Lincoln wrote the **Emancipation Proclamation** before the Civil War ended. This order freed slaves living in Confederate states. When the Union won the war, all Americans became free.

- This statue is in Washington, D.C. It was built in 1876. It shows President Lincoln freeing a slave.

DID YOU KNOW?

Some freed slaves left the plantations they were working at right away and moved to other places in North America. Others stayed and were paid for their work.

When the war was over, there were no telephones or televisions to spread the news. African-American slaves living in Texas were the last to find out about their freedom.

On June 18, 1865, Union general, Gordon Granger (below), arrived in Galveston, Texas, to take control of the state and enforce the emancipation of the slaves. It is said that on June 19, he read an order that stated all slaves were free. This day from then on became known as Juneteenth. Many slaves, however, did not hear about their freedom until days later when plantation owners read the order to them.

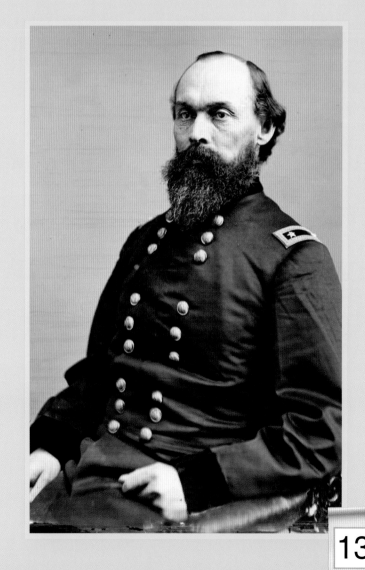

Juneteenth Customs

Parades are a popular Juneteenth custom.

On Juneteenth, people celebrate with **customs** that get handed down year after year. People of all backgrounds celebrate the end of slavery in the United States. They **honor** the African Americans' struggle for freedom.

DID YOU KNOW?

Pageants are a popular custom for Juneteenth celebrations. Every year a "Miss Juneteenth" is chosen. Some pageants also choose a younger "Little Miss Juneteenth."

"Miss Juneteenth" and "Little Miss Juneteenth" throw candies to the crowds.

One custom is to dress in fancy clothing for Juneteenth events. Before Juneteenth, many states had laws about what slaves could and could not wear. Many were not allowed to wear fancy clothing. When they were freed, they could wear what they wanted.

Juneteenth Music

At Juneteenth celebrations, people enjoy listening to music. Blues, gospel, and jazz music are often performed at Juneteenth celebrations. These kinds of music are played because they honor African-American musicians.

- Instruments such as the saxophone and trumpet are often used in jazz music. This girl is playing the saxophone.

Jazz music was first created over 100 years ago by African-American musicians. Some of the rhythms and sounds used are a bit like African music. Music festivals all across the United States, such as the Jazz Festival, are held to celebrate Juneteenth.

Live bands are common at Juneteenth celebrations.

DID YOU KNOW?

Since 1979, June is also Black Music Month in the United States. Music festivals celebrate both Juneteenth and African-American musicians at this time.

17

Juneteenth Foods

Juneteenth happens in late spring when the weather is warm. Many people celebrate by gathering outdoors for a picnic or a barbecue cookout. Some of the first Juneteenth gatherings held almost 150 years ago were celebrated in this way.

Families and friends often gather together for picnics on Juneteenth.

DID YOU KNOW?

*Strawberry soda pop is a **traditional** drink at Juneteenth food gatherings.*

• Hamburgers are a popular food at Juneteenth barbecues.

Picnics are often done potluck-style, where every family brings food to share. Often, lamb, pork, or beef is barbecued.

Some people hold fancy dinner parties and **banquets**. Guest speakers are invited to talk about African-American history.

Juneteenth Rodeos

BILL PICKETT

After Juneteenth, many freed slaves became cowboys. Cowboys were paid to work on large farms called ranches. Part of their job was to move cattle while riding horseback.

In 1994, the U.S. Postal Service made a special Bill Pickett stamp as part of the "Legends of the West" series.

DID YOU KNOW?

Bill Pickett was a famous cowboy who performed at rodeos over 100 years ago. He was the first African American to be honored at the National Cowboy Hall of Fame.

Rodeos are cowboy shows. Cowboys display their riding and roping skills. Rodeos are held to celebrate Juneteenth in many states. An annual Juneteenth Black Rodeo has been celebrated in a different U.S. city every year for over 16 years.

The Black Rodeo is a fun event held to celebrate Juneteenth.

Learning on Juneteenth

On Juneteenth, people take time to learn more about African-American history and **culture**. Special guests are invited to speak at Juneteenth gatherings. People of all backgrounds come to listen to the speakers to learn more about African-American culture.

These people are gathered in Florida to listen to a speaker on Juneteenth.

DID YOU KNOW?

African-American men were allowed to vote in 1870. At Juneteenth gatherings during that time, African-Americans were taught about their voting rights.

Juneteenth festivals show artwork and crafts by African Americans. Some Juneteenth festivals also have poetry readings. Some have booths where people can learn about issues such as health. People hold **workshops** that others can learn from.

Many Juneteenth festivals have displays set up with historical posters or books about African Americans.

Juneteenth in Texas

Today, people of all backgrounds travel to Texas on Juneteenth to celebrate the freedom of African Americans. After the emancipation of slaves was announced, many freed slaves bought land in Texas.

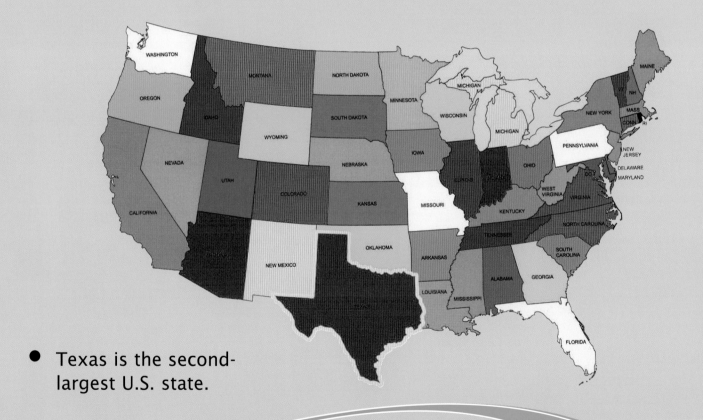

- Texas is the second-largest U.S. state.

DID YOU KNOW?

Juneteenth is sometimes called Emancipation Day in Texas.

Large Juneteenth celebrations take place throughout Texas every year.

In 1872, African Americans bought a 10-acre (four-hectare) piece of land in Houston, Texas, for $800. They bought the land so they could celebrate Juneteenth there every year. In 1896, a group of freed slaves bought 30 acres (12 hectares) of land that is now called Booker T. Washington State Park.

Juneteenth in Other States

Juneteenth is celebrated throughout other states, too. Many communities, both large and small, take part in events that celebrate the freedom of all U.S. **citizens**. In Denver, Colorado, an **annual** Juneteenth celebration has been held for over 30 years.

Singers perform at a Juneteenth celebration in Arizona.

DID YOU KNOW?

Many libraries, schools, and post offices have Juneteenth displays to celebrate the holiday.

The Birmingham Civil Rights Institute from Alabama takes part in the Juneteenth celebrations.

People watch a Juneteenth parade and other kinds of entertainment. They eat different foods, and visit booths with crafts and **information**.

In Long Beach, California, people go to Martin Luther King, Jr. Park and take part in an outdoor festival. People bring blankets and picnic lunches and watch and listen to entertainers perform for Juneteenth.

A Public Holiday

A public holiday is a special day that is celebrated by people within a state. Some people get the day off from school or work. In the United States, each state celebrates different public holidays.

• Lawmaker, Al Edwards, (shown here) made Juneteenth a legal holiday in Texas.

DID YOU KNOW?

Texas was the first state to celebrate Juneteenth as a paid public holiday in 1980.

In some states, such as Texas and Milwaukee, Juneteenth is a public holiday. Many states, such as California and Ohio, make Juneteenth a state holiday observance. This means that it is celebrated, but people do not get time off from work or school.

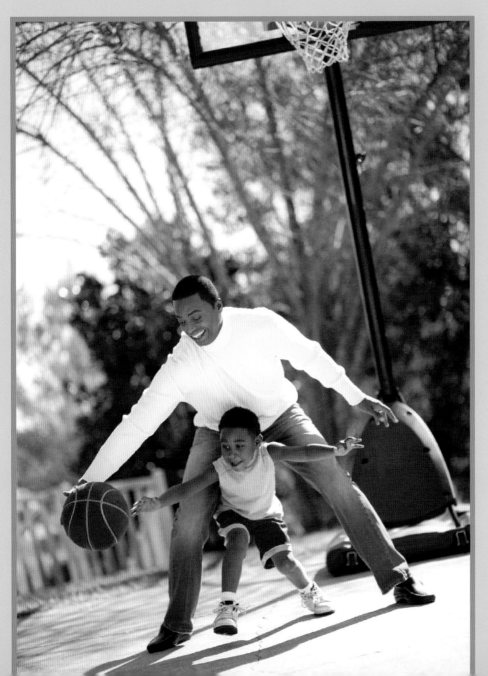

• Some states get Juneteenth off to have fun with friends and family and participate in Juneteenth activities.

29

Juneteenth Quiz

1. What was the last U.S. state to learn that all slaves were to be freed?

2. What two words make up Juneteenth?

3. Which U.S. president wrote the Emancipation Proclamation?

- Juneteenth is a good day to learn about African-American history.

DID YOU KNOW?

Famous American writer, Ralph Ellison, wrote a book called Juneteenth. *It was published five years after he died, in 1999.*

Juneteenth is a day to celebrate freedom!

4. What was the General's name who set the last slaves free in Texas?

5. How do people celebrate Juneteenth?

Glossary

ancestor A relative from your past

annual Occurring once a year

banquet A formal dinner often held in honor of someone or something

citizen A person who belongs to a country

culture The beliefs and habits shared by a group of people

custom A habit practiced by a group of people that is handed down from generation to generation

Emancipation Proclamation An order written by President Lincoln in 1863 that said that slaves living in Confederate States should be set free

Europe A continent of many countries between the Atlantic Ocean and Asia

freedom To be free to do as one chooses

honor Respect shown for a person or occasion

information What is learned from studying a subject

overcrowded Not having enough room

plantation A large farm where crops are grown

survive To be alive

traditional Something based on a custom

workshop An educational program that focuses on a topic or skill

Index